the little book of
LUNAR
BLESSINGS

MIX
Paper | Supporting
responsible forestry
FSC® C004800

Published in 2024 by OH!
An Imprint of Welbeck Non-Fiction Limited,
part of Welbeck Publishing Group.
Offices in: London – 20 Mortimer Street, London W1T 3JW
and Sydney – Level 17, 207 Kent St, Sydney NSW 2000 Australia
www.welbeckpublishing.com

ISBN 978-1-80069-561-0

Editorial consultant: Katalin Patnaik
Editorial: Victoria Denne
Project manager: Russell Porter
Production: Jess Brisley

A CIP catalogue record for this book is available from the British Library

Printed in Dubai

10 9 8 7 6 5 4 3 2 1

the little book of
LUNAR
BLESSINGS

Katalin Patnaik

CONTENTS

INTRODUCTION

No matter where in the world we look, the Moon has played an important role in human civilization from the beginning of time.

From aboriginal Australia to modern Christianity, the Moon is a constant in the rituals and daily lives of everyone on the planet.

Before Julius Caesar adopted a solar calendar and spread it all over the Roman Empire, and eventually the Western world, most cultures calculated months and years based on the phases of the Moon.

From a non-astrologer's point of view, it was easier and more efficient to follow the cyclical waxing and waning of the Moon than to calculate the Sun's angle in the sky.

In fact, many cultures still have a lunar calendar today. They might be using the "official", Gregorian calendar for everyday business, but important life events and festivals are still marked in the traditional lunar one.

Hindus, Buddhists, Confucianists, Taoists, Jews and Muslims all regularly use lunar or lunisolar calendars.

Have you ever wondered why Easter is always on a different date?

It is because it's calculated based on the Moon: Easter is the Sunday after the first full moon after the Spring Equinox in March.

It is the same reason why Hindu festivals like Holi and Diwali are always on different dates, too.

It can be an interesting shift in our perception to realize that these festivals actually are on the same day every year, and it is our solar calendar that keeps differing from the "actual" date.

Holi is always on the full moon of the month called Phagun.

Diwali is always on the new moon day of Kartik month.

The Moon is always at the same exact position in the sky on these days; it's just the Sun that changes.

Apart from its evident religious importance, the Moon has a huge physiological effect on everything on Earth, especially anything that contains water.

The position of the Moon controls the tides, and it causes floods and draughts.

Many animals time their procreation
or migration based on the Moon,
and many use it as a compass.
Crustaceans, birds, fish, beetles; even
coral have been documented
to do so.

The human body is made of 60%
water. Is it then surprising that the
phases of the Moon should affect us
as well?

Legends and
beliefs around the
Full Moon's
transformational
power aren't
accidental.

If we pay attention to people's behaviour around us, we may notice that around Full Moon, we all have more energy, and more intense emotions. People can become more aggressive, which is easy to see in traffic on the roads.

The romantic gesture of proposing under the Full Moon isn't arbitrary, either: passion and desire run high at this time of the lunar cycle.

The Moon reflects light that it receives from the Sun. As it circles the Earth, rays of sunlight strike its surface and illuminate different portions of its face.

Let us now explore how we can harness this celestial power and transform ourselves into the best version we can be!

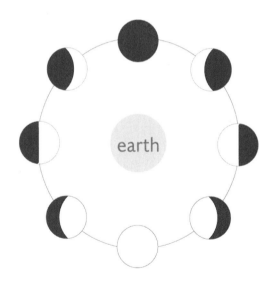

CHAPTER
1

MOON
LORE

In most cultures around the world, the Sun is associated with masculine, and the Moon with feminine, energies.

It is easy to see why: the Moon's cycle lasts 29 and a half days, about the same as a woman's menstrual cycle.

From time immemorial, the Moon symbolized that which is deep and hidden in the psyche: magic, intuition, sexuality, desires, dreams, deception and nightmares.

The Moon is the occult, which reveals itself only to those who seek it.

The Moon has three main phases: waxing, full, and waning.

This is represented by the archetypical figures of the Maiden, the Mother, and the Crone, together forming the Triple Goddess.

We find these figures in many cultures: the Norse Nornir; the Greek triad of Persephone, Demeter and Hecate; the list goes on.

Here you will find the most well-known Moon-related goddesses, and even a few Moon gods, with whom you might consider working in your practice.

GREEK MYTHS

Persephone, **Demeter** and **Hecate** together form the Greek Triple Goddess.

They represent the phases of the Moon: Persephone the New Moon, Demeter the Full Moon, and Hecate the Waning Moon.

PERSEPHONE
Roman: PROSERPINA

Daughter of Zeus and Demeter, wife of Hades, goddess of the Underworld and spring.

Persephone is one of the most multifaceted goddesses in Greek mythology.

Despite her being the goddess of spring, her name literally means "the destroyer".

Her legend says that one day she was plucking flowers in a garden, when Hades, the god of the Underworld, kidnapped her.

When Demeter came looking for her, Persephone had already eaten six pomegranate seeds offered to her by Hades and so she couldn't fully return with her mother to Earth.

Hades saw Demeter's grief upon losing her daughter, and so he agreed to let her spend six months with her mother, and six months in the Underworld.

Persephone returns to Demeter in spring, and goes back to her husband in winter.

She gradually fell in love with Hades, who treats her as an equal, and they rule the Underworld together.

- Her symbols are a sheaf of wheat and a torch.

- Her festival, along with her mother Demeter's, was the Thesmophoria. Offer her pomegranates, flowers, jewellery or grains.

- Associated scents are pomegranate, vanilla and spring flowers.

- Associated colours are green, pink and black.

DEMETER
Roman: CERES

Daughter of Rhea and Chronos,
goddess of agriculture and growth.
Demeter doesn't have a husband,
only lovers.

She had children with Iaison, Poseidon
and Zeus, with whom she conceived
Persephone.

When Persephone was kidnapped by Hades, Demeter was so distressed that she neglected her duties as a harvest goddess, and all plants wilted away on Earth.

Seeing this, Zeus helped her locate Persephone, and arranged a deal with Hades to return Demeter's daughter to the surface for six months each year.

When Persephone is back on the
surface of Earth, Demeter is happy,
and crops grow in abundance.

- Her symbols are the cornucopia,
  a sheaf of wheat, a torch, and
  poppies.

- Her festival was the Thesmophoria. Offer her fruits, bread, pork, mint and jewellery.

- Associated scents are spices like clove or cinnamon, summer and autumn flowers, and mint.

- Associated colours are green, black and gold.

HEKATE

Roman: TRIVIA

Daughter of Perses and Asteria, she is the goddess of crossroads, transformation, childbirth, witchcraft, ghosts and the Underworld.

According to legend, she helped Demeter search for Persephone and make a deal with Hades regarding Persephone's residence.

She is a virgin goddess, and she hasn't got a husband, although in some traditions she had children with some of her lovers.

Once, Hermes tried to rape her, but she roared at him and chased him away, earning her the name Brimo, which means "Angry".

What a goddess!

- Her symbols are dogs, keys, serpents and a torch.

- Her festival was Deipnon, and the days of 13 August and 30 November.

- Offer her candles, garlic, black coffee, black chocolate, honey and leeks.

- Associated scents are honey, lemon, cinnamon, myrrh and mint.

- Associated colours are black, purple and red.

SELENE

Roman: LUNA

Daughter of Hyperion and Theia,
wife of Endymion, the goddess of the
Moon. She can help you find love,
clarity and peace.

- Her symbols are a crescent moon, a bull, a chariot and a torch.

- Her festival is every full moon, and Mondays. Offer her cakes and cookies, confectionery and fruits.

- Associated scents are lavender, flowers and frankincense.

- Associated colours are white and silver.

NORSE MYTHS

It is interesting to note that in Norse myths, as well as in Egyptian and Indian lore, the Moon is represented by a male god.

In Norse mythology, the god of the Moon is **Mani**, and the goddess of the Sun is **Sol**, swapping the more usual gender roles around.

This is reflected in the German language, for example, where the Sun is feminine, "die Sonne", and the Moon is masculine, "der Mond".

the NORNIR

In Norse myths, the Triple Goddess is present in the form of the three Nornir (singular Norn), who decide the fates of mortals.

Their names are **Urd**, **Skuld** and **Verdandi**. They are giantesses who live at the trunk of the World Tree Yggdrasil, and water it from their sacred well to keep it alive.

They see past, present and future, and shape destinies. Urd is the Crone, Skuld is the Mother, and Verdandi is the Maiden aspect.

They were not worshipped in Viking times, but people have started to work with them in the last few decades.

They help with cutting cords, thread work, ancestral and spirit work.

- Their symbols are a web and a spinning wheel.

- Their festival is the first night of Yule, Mothers' Night.

- Offer them any handmade fibre art, porridge, or the act of cleaning a house.

- Associated scents are myrrh, nag champa, amber and musk.

- Associated colours are black, grey and white.

MANI

He is the god of the Moon, and the brother of Sol, the Sun goddess.

Mani and Sol are the children of Mundilfari, who, according to legend, was really proud of his children, and said they were as brilliant as the Sun and the Moon.

The gods were angered by his pride, so they kidnapped Mani and Sol, to make them the deities of the celestial bodies.

Mani drives his chariot across the skies at night, followed by two children, a boy, Hjuki, and a girl, Bil.

According to legend, Hjuki and Bil were one night walking home from a well, where they were sent to by their abusive parents. Mani saw them, and took them with him to forever follow him around in the sky.

Hjuki represents the growing aspect of the Moon, while Bil is the waning period.

Mani brings protection and good dreams.

- His symbols are the Moon, an axe and a pole.

- His festival is the third night of Yule. Offer him cookies, flowers that bloom at night, water and the act of fasting.

- Associated scents are mint, vanilla and jasmine.

- Associated colours are blue, silver, black and purple.

FREYJA

Daughter of Njord, Freyja is the goddess of love, fertility, magic, and war.

Many people are aware of Valhalla, where Odin receives slain warriors, but have you heard of Sessrumnir?

Freyja and Odin share the souls of
fallen warriors equally.

After riding over the battlefields
on her chariot pulled by cats,
Freyja receives her share of souls in
Sessrumnir, the "hall of many seats".

Freyja is associated with the Full Moon and Friday is named after her.

- Her symbols are cats, falcons, and her necklace the Brisingamen.

- Her festival is the first night of Yule, or any Friday.

- Offer her honey, mead, flowers, jewellery and perfume.

- Associated scents are rose, sandalwood and cypress.

- Associated colours are gold, white and yellow.

HINDU
MYTHS

CHANDRA

Again, we have an exception: Chandra is the god of the Moon. He gives beauty and intelligence.

According to legend, Chandra had 27 wives, but he favoured Rohini above all the others. All his wives were sisters, and when they went to their father, Daksh, to complain, Daksh cursed Chandra to wither away and die.

The other gods knew that if the Moon disappeared, it would have catastrophic effects on Earth, so they ran to Lord Shiva, one of the Hindu trinity, for help.

Shiva didn't see it right to completely remove the curse, but he blessed Chandra so that just before he died, he would slowly regain his strength and become healthy again – only to lose it and die, over and over again, forever.

- His symbols are a rope and a chariot pulled by an antelope.

- His festival is every Monday, or every night right after the new moon.

- Offer him water, yoghurt, butter or milk.

- Associated scents are camphor, sandalwood, jasmine and mogra.

- Associated colour is white.

TRIDEVI

The Triple Goddess can be interpreted in two ways in Hinduism.

It can be made up of Lakshmi, the goddess of wealth, Sarasvati, the goddess of knowledge and arts, and Shakti, the goddess of power.

At the same time, the concept can be interpreted to the different aspects of Shakti: Sati as the Maiden, Parvati or Durga as the Mother, and Kali as the Crone.

LAKSHMI

Goddess of wealth, wife of Vishnu.

- Her symbols are the lotus flower, gold coins and owls.

- Her festival is Laksmi Puja, around November.

- Offer her saffron paste, Kumkum powder or jewellery.

- Associated scents are lotus, sandalwood and flowers.

- Associated colours are red and gold.

SARASVATI

Goddess of knowledge and arts, wife of Brahma.

- Her symbols are swans, books, and the Vedas.

- Her festival is Sarasvati Puja, around February.

- Offer her fruits and confectionery.

- Associated scents are jasmine and patchouli.

- Associated colours are white and gold.

SHAKTI

Goddess of power, wife of Shiva.

- Her symbols are the lotus flower and weapons, especially the trident and the sword.

- Her festivals are the two Navaratri, around October and April.

- Offer her fruits, honey, and milk products.

- Associated scents are sandalwood and flowers.

- Associated colours are red, green and orange.

SATI

Daughter of Daksh and Prasuti, first wife of Shiva, goddess of fidelity, longevity and happy marriages.

She was so fiercely loyal to, and in love with, her husband Shiva, that when her father, Daksh, insulted him in front of her, Sati threw away her life, proclaiming she couldn't bear the humiliation of living as the daughter of Daksh any longer. She later reincarnated as Parvati.

- Her symbol is the sacrificial fire. She is often shown sitting in a sacred firepit, or her burned corpse being carried by the mourning Shiva.

- Her festivals are the two Navaratri, around October and April.

- Offer her flowers, fruits, and confectionery.

- Associated scents are sandalwood and musk.

- Associated colours are white, yellow and orange.

PARVATI

Daughter of Himavan and Minavati, second wife of Shiva, the mother goddess.

Sati reincarnated as Parvati, who, from early childhood, felt a strong connection to Shiva. Despite Shiva spending all his time in mournful meditation, Parvati managed to enchant him with her deep love and innocence. Their marriage anniversary is celebrated every year on Maha Shivratri.

- Her symbols are her children and her husband, the lotus flower and the trident.

- Her festivals are the two Navaratri, around October and April, Durga Puja.

- Offer her flowers, confectionery, vegetarian food or rice.

- Associated scents are musk and sandalwood.

- Associated colours are green, white and red.

KALI

A form of Parvati, wife of Shiva, goddess of war, anger, destruction, and time.

According to legend, a demon named Raktabeej terrorized the three realms. No one could defeat him, because wherever his blood spilled, another demon sprung up to fight. When all seemed lost, Kali appeared and drank up every drop of Raktabeej's blood, consumed all the cloned demons, and defeated their army.

- Her symbols are skulls, severed heads, blood, swords sickles and tridents.

- Her festivals are the two Navaratri, around October and April, and Kali Puja.

- Offer her red hibiscus flowers, food including fish and mutton, but never beef.

- Associated scents are hibiscus and rose.

- Associated colours are red and black.

EGYPTIAN
MYTHS

KHONSU

Falcon-headed god of the Moon, Khonsu marks the passage of time, and heals and protects those who worship him.

- His symbols are the moon disc, the ankh and the falcon head.

- His festival is Heb Nefer En Inet, the Beautiful Festival of the Valley.

- Offer him figs, grapes, dates, bread and meat.

- Associated scents are myyrh, juniper, cypress, saffron and mint.

- Associated colours are white and green.

ISIS

Wife of Osiris, mother of Horus, goddess of love, fertility, healing, magic and the Full Moon.

Isis and Osiris had been ruling over the other gods, until one day Set killed Osiris, and cut his body into pieces. Afterwards, Isis embarked on a long journey to locate all of the pieces. She sewed them back together, and conceived Horus with the body.

Horus grew up and restored order by defeating Set.

Osiris, his soul revived by receiving a proper funeral, remained in the Underworld, and became the god of the Afterlife.

- Her symbols are cow horns, the moon disc and wings.

- Her festival is Amesysia.

- Offer her sycamore seeds, jewellery, confectionery, raisins and fruits.

- Associated scents are frankincense, myrrh and cinnamon.

- Associated colours are white and green.

WORKING with GODS and GODDESSES

This is not as hard as it first sounds. They are supernatural beings, infinitely older and more powerful than us mortals, and they deserve respect and caution, that is true. But most of them are really approachable.

When you work with deities, you give them offerings, gifts; you give them a small part of your energy.

And, in exchange for that, they will be able to help you with your supernatural dealings, and your everyday life, too.

Before asking any deity for help, build rapport with them.

If you don't have an established relationship with a deity and you are going to call on them, they are not likely to rush to your aid. Make sure you get to know them first, spend some time with them.

Show your devotion and appreciation, and then you can ask for favours.

Deities can have many types of different relationships with us mortals, ranging from being worshipped gods, to mentors, friends, found family and even lovers.

Spend time figuring out which deity you feel most drawn to, and start making offerings to them.

Listen to the feelings you get when you think about them. That is the kind of relationship you will have. But be careful and stay grounded.

It can sometimes be hard to tell reality from fantasy. Learning a form of divination, or asking a professional, can help with discernment.

Decorate your altar with things associated with your chosen deity.

If you chose Shakti, a statue of any of her forms should be easy enough to come by – although Kali might be too intense for beginners, so unless you really feel called, start with Durga instead.

Look for a statue that really speaks to you.

If you are on a budget, print out a picture of your chosen deity, or, even better, draw your own and place that on the altar.

You could include their symbols, their favourite things, their family, or things that remind you of them.

If you don't know what to offer, just a white candle, a cup of water, some fruits and sandalwood incense stick should do the trick for any deity.

If you need to hide your practice,
you can skip having an altar altogether,
or make it tiny to fit into a small,
inconspicuous box.

As an offering, a piece of fresh fruit is
great. Wash it, close your eyes, focus
your intent on giving it to your chosen
deity, and after offering it up like this,
eat it. No one needs to know apart
from you and your deity.

With time, you will feel called to include different offerings, and you could do your research on the internet about what each deity likes, too.

Neo-pagan witch websites are abundant with personal experiences you could draw inspiration from. The lists above are only meant as a suggestion to start with.

After making your offering, spend some time thinking and meditating on your deity. Tell them you are grateful for their presence and would like to work with them.

Ask for a sign that they agree to work with you. The more specific you make it, the better.

If you choose Freyja, for example, you could ask for three identical feathers to be sent your way. Alternatively, it could be a dream, a certain number that pops up all the time; anything you like.

Keep your eyes out for your sign, and trust that you will know when you see it.

Don't be disheartened if you don't receive a sign straight away.

Keep trying until you succeed or it becomes clear that the specific deity doesn't want to work with you – in which case, usually another deity pops up out of nowhere.

CHAPTER

2

WHAT are LUNAR BLESSINGS?

Lunar blessings are rituals to connect you to the Moon's power, and harness it for your goals.

The Moon has always been associated with magic and transformation, and with lunar blessings, you can transform your life into what you want it to be.

That is not all!

Since time immemorial, people knew exactly what task needed to be done at what exact moon phase.

For example, sawing wood needs to be done in the waxing phase. Weeding and thinning plants has to be done while the moon is waning. Bread rises better while the moon is waxing, while renovating is best done while the moon is waxing crescent.

Following such instructions ensures the best outcome.

The specific zodiac sign that the Moon passes through also makes its mark on the Moon's energy.

The fiery New Moon in Aries has very different vibrations to the gentle New Moon in Cancer.

Working with a Moon deity helps maximize this celestial power, and makes it easier to focus your energy on your rituals.

Working with deities also makes it easier to form a habit of living magically, and to keep your goals for your blessings at the front of your mind.

When using
Lunar Blessings,
all of these aspects
are combined,
and bring clarity,
focus and magic
into your life.

To effectively use Lunar Blessings,
we need to learn the Moon's phases
and what they are associated with.

Align yourself to the world's rhythm
to maximize your potential.

CHAPTER

3

the PHASES

of the MOON

the first phase
the NEW MOON

This is the phase when the Moon is not illuminated by the Sun, and is barely visible in the sky. It lasts one to three nights.

The New Moon is the best time to release what doesn't serve you anymore, have a self-care day, or banish any negative presence from your life.

the second phase

WAXING CRESCENT

This is the phase when the Moon looks like a crescent that will grow into the letter D.

It lasts for about 6 nights.

Waxing Crescent is the time of rejuvenation and rebirth. Set new intentions, new goals and new plans at this time of the month.

the third phase

the FIRST
QUARTER

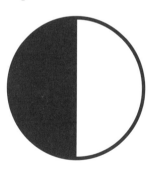

This is the phase when the Moon looks like the letter D.

It lasts one night.

The First Quarter is the time to implement your new plans, make the first real step and overcome obstacles.

the fourth phase

WAXING
GIBBOUS

This is the phase when the Moon looks like something between the letters D and O; almost full. It lasts for about 6 nights.

Waxing Gibbous is the time to reassess the viability of your plans and make amendments. It's a good time to reflect on where you are in life, and where you want to be.

the fifth phase

FULL MOON

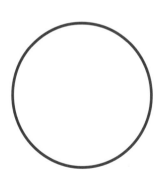

This is the phase when the Moon is a complete circle in the sky, fully illuminated by the Sun. It lasts one night.

A Full Moon is the best time to count your blessings, do manifestation work, publish a new project, celebrate and show gratitude.

the sixth phase

WANING
GIBBOUS

This is the phase when the Moon starts to disappear, and from an O it slowly becomes a C. It lasts for about 6 nights.

Waning Gibbous is the best time to move forward, and start setting new goals, to work for closures and think about the lessons learned. It's also a great time to share what you have with others and do charity or volunteer work.

the seventh phase

the THIRD
QUARTER

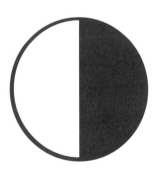

This is the phase when the Moon
looks like a flipped-over letter D.
It lasts one night.

The Third Quarter is the best time
to forgive anyone who has hurt you,
including yourself, and to reconnect
with your higher self. It is the time to
move on from the past and enjoy
what you have.

the eighth phase

WANING
CRESCENT

This is the phase when the Moon looks like a letter C. It lasts for about 6 nights.

Waning Crescent is the best time for releasing the past and banishing any negative influence. It's the period of rest and recuperation, and surrendering yourself to a higher power in matters out of your control, before the cycle starts again.

IN SHORT:

The waxing, growing Moon is the time to do blessings for growth and new beginnings.

The Full Moon is best for lending extra power to your blessings, so be sure to focus on big, important things at this time.

The Waning Moon is best for banishing and releasing, as well as spiritual work.

The New Moon is the phase for inner work, banishing and bringing justice.

ZODIAC SIGNS

To further strengthen your blessing's power, you could consider timing it with the signs of the Zodiac.

Here is a list of which Zodiac signs correspond to which area of life.

Moon in Aries is best for new starts and self-confidence.

Moon in Taurus is best to deal with money and property, abundance and sensual pleasures.

Moon in Gemini is best for communication, creative writing and technology.

Moon in Cancer is best focused on family life, fertility, healing and forgiveness.

Moon in Leo is suited for networking, building rapport, performing for others and confidence.

Moon in Virgo is best for service, healing and selflessness.

Moon in Libra is the time for mediation, diplomacy, arts and studies.

Moon in Scorpio is well suited for spicing up your sex life, strengthening allegiances and unveiling secrets.

Moon in Sagittarius is great for travel, re-examining your beliefs and ethics and the excitement of novelty.

Moon in Capricorn is the best time for business matters, perseverance and discipline.

Moon in Aquarius is the best time for creative projects and reinventing yourself.

Moon in Pisces is the time for spirituality, shadow work and magic.

CHAPTER
4

PREPARING
for the
BLESSINGS

Always start with physically cleansing your surroundings.

On the day when you plan to do your blessing, clean your house as deeply as you are able to. Dust the shelves, mop the floor, remove the cobwebs.

Pay extra attention to areas connected to your blessing.

If you are about to do a blessing for family harmony, make the living room extra tidy. If you want to manifest a lover, it's your bedroom you need to make sure is spotless.

For a new car, spend time clearing up the garage first.

Cleanse all tools that you are planning to use. Any candles, offerings, incense or smudge sticks should be prepared beforehand.

Take a nice bath with essential oils and bath salts. Wash your hair and focus on the water's cleansing properties. If you can't take a bath, a shower is just as effective.

Use your favourite soap. You could even buy one of those handmade magical soaps, or make your own for these special occasions.

Put on clean clothes. Every piece should be freshly washed.

If you have ceremonial clothes, you could wear those.

Cleanse the house and yourself
spiritually, too. There are many ways
you could do it.

Smudging, clearing away negative
energies with smoke, is a good way to
get rid of harmful, negative energies.

Nowadays, smudging with sage is very popular, but be aware that some of the sage available on the market has been harvested by poachers, so try to research your seller before you buy.

Using bay leaves, or dry red chillies for a thorough cleansing if you feel a stubborn negative force is around, are a lot cheaper, more ethical, and are just as effective.

Open all your windows so the negative energy has a way to leave the house.

In a fireproof bowl, light your smudge stick and slowly spread the smoke all over the house, walking from room to room, repeating your intention in your head or out loud: all negative energy leaves the house, and positivity replaces it.

Call in any gods, guides or angels you are working with, and ask them to stay and lend their help for your blessing.

After cleansing the house and yourself, you need to ground yourself, and ask for protection.

Sit down on the floor in the space you decided to perform the blessing. You could lie down if you are not able to sit. You should preferably be able to see the Moon from a window, or go outside if you can.

Close your eyes, and feel the ground under you. Imagine roots growing from your body, deep into the earth. All your worries, all your tension seeps away through them, and the earth transforms them into strength to act.

Visualize that strength entering your body, making you ready to do the work you set out to do.

Now visualize a bright burst of light starting from your chest, and filling the whole house, forming a protective sphere around it. Know that only those who you allow can enter through that light. Everything else stays outside.

Ask your gods and guides for protection. Draw your magic circle.

You are ready to do the blessing.

CHAPTER
5

BLESSINGS

It is always best to write your own blessings, because then you can make them as broad or as specific as you like. You can make them elaborate poems in praise of the Moon, or just a couple of sentences. It really is up to you.

The blessings in this chapter act as a framework, to showcase the tools you have learned earlier in this book. Adjust the blessings according to your requirements.

When you write your blessing, be as clear as possible in what you'd like to happen.

It is also a good idea to include the clause of "if it harms none".

the NEW MOON in ARIES

Self-confidence

Potent new moon, I embrace your blessings of empowerment tonight!

May your darkness resemble the darkness of the earth, where the planted seed germinates!

Protect this blessing, this seed of passion, this seed of fire, this seed of self-confidence and unwavering self-love!

On this New Moon in Aries, may all doubt abandon me, and may my inner warrior awaken!

May it grow in power as the Moon grows from a sliver to its full glory, and may it radiate from my being forever more!

Bless me so I am ready to embark on the journey ahead!

I call upon the warrior goddess Kali, to
show me my own strength, to guide
me into my power!

Fierce goddess, slay my demons of
doubt and fear, and replace them
with the flame of self-assuredness and
fearlessness!

So it is, so mote it be!

FULL MOON
in TAURUS

Abundance

Radiant Full Moon, generous
Universe, accept my gratitude for
what I have in my life!

May your light guide me to
appreciation and enjoyment of the
little pleasures.

Open my heart to gratefulness so
I can see my blessings clearly.

Luminous Full Moon in Taurus, grant me the wisdom and patience to tend to my wealth and grow it steadily.

Charge me with an abundance mindset, and remove shame from wanting wealth!

Help me learn to welcome prosperity into my life!

Generous Lakshmi, send
opportunities my way so I might
grow in wealth and wane in worries
for the mundane.

So it is, so mote it be!

WANING
CRESCENT MOON
in GEMINI

**Communication
and clear thinking**

Under the Waning Crescent
of the Moon in Gemini, I release
the thoughts that don't serve
me anymore.

Gentle Crescent, clear my mind
of clutter and intrusive thoughts
so I may move on to the
new phase with renewed vigour
and creative passion!

Help me to look inwards to explore
and understand myself better, with
an ever-growing understanding of the
world around me.

Bless me with the talent of clear
communication!

Gentle goddess Saraswati,
bless me with clear ideas and the
skill to bring them to life!

Hold my pen while I write,
bless my keyboard as I type, so I may
honour you through my work!

So it is, so mote it be!

WAXING MOON
in CANCER

Healing and harmony

Embraced by the restorative rays of
the Waxing Moon in Cancer, I ask for
healing and peace.

Bless me with the ability to forgive
those who wronged me, to love those
who love me, and to accept everyone
under the spectrum of the human
experience.

Teach me joy, teach me love, for others and for myself.

Bless me with harmony in my family, and emotional stability in my life.

Powerful Persephone, grant me
the courage to be myself, and bless
me with loved ones who accept
and nourish my authentic self for
what it is.

Protect me from people's sharp
tongues, and heal the wounds they
caused in the past.

So it is, so mote it be!

THIRD
QUARTER MOON
in LEO

Rightful
Pride

Illuminated by the Third Quarter Moon in Leo, I release self-doubt and my limiting beliefs.

I welcome this celestial blessing to take the place of shyness and fill me with radiant confidence in my authentic self.

I embody confidence and openness in my relationships, and share this divine spark with whoever I interact with.

I am ready to share myself with the world, and own my creative ideas and artwork with pride.

Wise Hekate, enable me to let go
of excess ego and pride, and find a
healthy balance to success!

So it is, so mote it be!

NEW MOON
in VIRGO

Service for others

Merciful Moon, always dutiful and
true, lend me your strength to remain
steadfast in my work.

Just like you continue your journey through the sky even when you're about to fade away, I too shall perform my duty through tough times.

And just like you regain your power in each cycle, I too shall see better days, and look back with pride on what I've accomplished.

Luminous Chandra, soothe my soul
with your gentle light.

Bless me with kindness and grace,
give strength to my heart so it may
remain gentle.

So it is, so mote it be!

NEW MOON
in LIBRA

Diplomacy and fairness

On this New Moon in Libra, I call upon
the power of Khonsu!

Wise and powerful god, bless me
with the skill of diplomacy so I may
settle my matters in a mutually
beneficial way.

Dearest Moon of negotiators, may
my disputes end with fair judgement
and healthy closure!

May we all learn justice from you,
and may we start all interaction with
clear intentions.

FULL MOON
in SCORPIO

◯

Fierce loyalty

Mystical Full Moon, bless me with
your light! Infuse me with your
steadfastness, envelop me in your
resolve to do what is right!

Oh Moon in Scorpio, I bare my soul
to you. See the unwavering loyalty
I hold to my cause!

The stars may fade, the Sun may burn
out, but this determination will never
cease to blaze in my heart!
Oh Goddess Sati, bear witness to my
faithfulness, and bless me so I might
embody your fierce devotion!

So it is, so mote it be!

WANING
CRESCENT MOON
in SAGITTARIUS

Courage and fairness

Shimmering Crescent of the Moon,
grant me the courage and drive I need
for this new journey ahead!

Ignite the fire of excitement and
adventure, and bless me with
confidence and energy to see it
through!

May this waxing moon in
Sagittarius open my mind to new
perspectives, and give me the bravery
to look within and see where
I need to work on myself!

Bless me with unending curiosity
and acceptance!

May I remain non-judgemental
towards myself and others!

So it is, so mote it be!

WANING GIBBOUS MOON in CAPRICORN

Resolve and rationality

May this Waning Gibbous Moon in
Capricorn bless me with the patience,
discipline and determination of this
Zodiac sign!

May it help me release what no longer
serves me!

Old dreams that couldn't become,
old ambitions that hold me back, set
me free so I can reach my potential!

So it is, so mote it be!

FULL MOON in AQUARIUS

Impact
on the world

Glorious Moon, beloved of poets,
muse of artists! Charge me with
your power, infuse me with your
creative genius!

Bless me so I may express my deepest
thoughts and emotions! Let me make
my mark in this world, let me find
connections with others you have
gifted with the passion of art!

May my art act as a catalyst for healing
and progress in the world!
Bless my art, muse of muses!

So it is, so mote it be!

NEW MOON
in PISCES

Shadow work

Under the protection of the New Moon, I look inside and face my shadow self. I see myself for who I am, and I finally embrace it. I grieve for the parts that hurt; I rage for the parts that were betrayed. I accept my flaws and celebrate my strengths.

Magical New Moon of Pisces, bless me with insight! Bless me with discernment and help me grow into what my higher self is whispering to me!

So it is, so mote it be!

CHAPTER
6

SUPPORTING
TECHNIQUES

Journaling is a great way to document where you started, and how the blessing is affecting your life.

It can be helpful to look back after some time and see how things have changed since you started.

Affirmations are brilliant for exactly what their name suggests: to reaffirm your intentions.

You have done the blessing, now you can reinforce it every day until it manifests, and beyond.

Write an affirmation for your blessing that you can repeat every morning.

Make your affirmation simple and positive, for example:

I am successful!

The gods are with me!

I love my body as it is,
and I take good care of it!

I am strong!

The gods are with me!

I can do this!

Guided meditations on specific subjects you are working on reinforce your focus on your goals.

They can help you achieve the mindset needed to overcome any obstacles and manifest your desires.

Journeying can also be really rewarding and instructional.

Use an image of the Moon to inspire you. It could be a tarot card, or a painting or photo of the Moon, or an associated deity.

Pay attention to each detail, and close your eyes.

Imagine yourself stepping into the
scene depicted on the picture.

Let your imagination run wild, and
when your adventure is done, note
it down to analyse later.

Moon bathing – just like a good sunbathing session can rejuvenate you, moon bathing will fill your body and soul with the energy of the Moon.

If you can't see the Moon from the room you have performed your blessing in, go outside and let the rays of the Moon hold you in their gentle embrace.

Leave your magical items out to moon-bathe on Full Moon nights.

Spread out your tarot cards, your crystals, or any other items you use in your practice, and leave them on the windowsill for the night to recharge.

May your journey
be blessed
by the Moon!

So it is,
and so mote it be!